ROSE ASH
SAMUEL A. ADEYEMI

This is a work of fiction. All names, characters, places, and incidents are a product of the author's imagination. Any resemblance to real events or persons, living or dead, is entirely coincidental.

Published by Akashic Books
©2023 Samuel A. Adeyemi
ISBN: 978-1-63614-130-5

All rights reserved
Printed in China
First printing

Akashic Books
Brooklyn, New York
Instagram, Twitter, Facebook:
@AkashicBooks
E-mail: info@akashicbooks.com
Website: www.akashicbooks.com

African Poetry Book Fund
Prairie Schooner
University of Nebraska
110 Andrews Hall
Lincoln, Nebraska 68588

TABLE OF CONTENTS

Preface by Patricia Jabbeh Wesley 5

Flight 7
The Ladder 8
Inception 9
Penury 10
For Mohmoh 13
The Clocks 14
Applying Psalms 121 to an Unbeliever 16
Homecoming 18
White Noise Apartment 19
Fear Is the Boy's Savior 22
Hypothesis 23
Tongues 25
Surrendering to Joy 26

Acknowledgments 28

PREFACE
by Patricia Jabbeh Wesley

Samuel A. Adeyemi's chapbook *Rose Ash* is a brilliant, bitingly honest, and powerful piece of work—an art within an art form of its own making. From page to page, every line takes us by the hand into the underworld of the living and the dead, lifting every dead leaf, every dead twig or limb, piece by piece, as if this poet were a clergyman himself, or a student of the Bible. He takes on not only the Bible, but also our understanding of deity, asking all the questions we would have loved to have asked by his age. *Rose Ash* reminds me of a young person so wise that the elders in Africa would take one look at him, or hear him speak, and say, "This is not a child at all, or a young man, but one of our ancestors coming back to earth to reprimand us or teach us the lessons we should have learned long ago."

Rose Ash boldly takes the reader on a journey as it explores deity and the underworld of the dead, and wrestles with questions of life and death and tradition. In the first lines of the first poem, "Flight," Adeyemi's speaker quickly warns us by opening the door to his world in lines like, "I live inside a plummet. / Limbs in constant flutter for balance, / feet searching for earth, remembering / the days the Psalms comforted me— / *He set my feet upon a rock.* / If the butterfly could speak, it would tell you / its nightmare is bending back to a caterpillar, / that thing empty of grace."

These poems have the audacity to question faith, Christianity, and religion as we know it, allowing each line, each metaphor, each powerful rendering of every sound, every beat, every freedom of tone, buried inside each piece, to make the reader feel and see what the speaker, and yes, the poet has seen. Speaker after speaker in *Rose Ash* invites us to dissect our faith, to stand up to not just the ways in which we believe, or understand tradition, family, life, and death, but also the unusual ways we find unbelief as a source of healing. In his poem, "Hypothesis," Adeyemi's speaker evokes the questions we wrestle with about the afterlife, heaven, hell, where we go when we die, and the hypotheses we have formed about the afterlife. Here, the speaker tells us that "the prophet's wife says / tribulation is the heirloom of the earth; / only in heaven shall we find eternal peace," and in response to this assertion by the prophet's wife, the speaker proclaims the unexpected, "Invention: heaven is wherever I say it is."

Such boldness in a chapbook typically occurs after a poet has had decades to understand life and poetry and the power a poem wields on the page and after the page. But Adeyemi has refused to wait. Perhaps, this is because in all of his profound use of language, the powerful symbolism in the images he employs, there is a deep feeling of pain he wants us to understand. His deeply felt language in this powerful collection is a subtle exploration of pain, as is his call for urgency in overcoming pain if one is to survive.

Rose Ash reminds us of both a journey and the road the journey must negotiate to get home. The poet concludes that "Fear Is the Boy's Savior." The voice behind each speaker's story not only surprises but also alerts us to what is in store from such a talented and gifted poet.

FLIGHT

I live inside a plummet.
Limbs in constant flutter for balance,

feet searching for earth, remembering
the days the Psalms comforted me—

He set my feet upon a rock.
If the butterfly could speak, it would tell you

its nightmare is bending back to a caterpillar,
that thing empty of grace. This is the song

of the cast away. The boy whose miracles
fell in reverse—wine into water, water

becoming thirst. I levitate toward bethel
and it ends with wings returning

to a shoulder. I soar:
I fall back into the mouth of my silence.

I fall like a flower, like rain.
I fall like a bird obeying an arrow.

THE LADDER

Forfeit it all if you've come looking for
God. This was the same place I lost him.
There is nothing here, but the absence
of the spirit. The Father and his grace
departed years ago. Perhaps if you cut

me open, a whit of light may still
sear your skin. But do not mistake the light
of God for God. The souvenir is accidental.
He once dwelt within these temple walls,
singing from the valley

of my voice. Come look into the tomb of
my bones. He is not here. He is risen
from me and even the angels followed him.
I promise, I tried to make them stay.
We wrestled, skin against the opposite

of skin. I pulled them by their abundance
of white, but when they turned and looked
into my face, I had no choice but to let them
go. My friend, I tried. There were blisters
sprouting around my eyes. I was blind

for half a decade. I basked within a shadow.
It was hell but lonelier. I could not see
my flames. Dear darkness, did you
know this? I could not see my flames.
I guessed they were blue.

INCEPTION

The women from my tribe used to shave their
heads to mourn their husbands. The razor through

tufts of blood. I do not know why I tell you this.
I am not the wife of any family's dead.

What I'm trying to say is, *listen*. The elegies
keep following me to sleep. It happened again

last night. When Father died, he didn't. I awoke
after the dream, ran to his room. I looked at him.

His chest widening with breath. *Good morning,*
I said. *You're alive* was what I meant.

You could hear it, the gratitude flooding my
voice. Not to God, but to the wonder of God.

Mother asked me later what I saw in my sleep.
I sang her the elegies. She began to pray against

the spirit of death. In my tribe, the word *ala*
translates to dream. In Igbo, it loosely means

the goddess of death. What I'm trying to say is,
loss begins at the precipice of language.

At the threshold of another tongue, the people
I love are not alive to see me love them.

PENURY

All I am known for is desire and thirst.
                                       I want to be

the object of want.
If I could, I would pull out a river

                         from my right eye,
         just so the other watches in envy.

Look, little iris, I would say.
Lust after me.

                 And of course it will. The hunger
                    of the flesh is for the flesh.

A lover's open mouth trembles
for another open mouth.

                         Likewise, I am doing it;
             opening to the grace of the world,

hoping it would someday enter me
like a lance made only of light.

                     And what did God say to my lack?
                   Take the vines of your sorrow

and make from it a garland.
Holy Father, my sorrow is sexless.

                I do not know how to touch it.
                Last time, I burned the flowers.

Behold, my fingers still smell
the rose-ash.

                I have spent so much time
        unlearning the mechanics of religion.

I have turned myself inside out.
I sat next to it, my open skin,

                scraping the names of God
            from my bones, like a thumb

invading a line of seeds.
You would think I am not

                      prodigal enough to
                return to His feet, my heart

hardened like a wreath
of two spines. But I know

                    the roads back to God;
             when I reached the shore of

His joy, He was the water
washing it away.

      See, I did not choose my void.
        If the angels want me, I will

let them pull me by the jaw,
my body ascending into heaven.

        There is no greater absence
      than this—I know the miracles

I want, I know I cannot
hold them. May something

                find me and kiss the rim
                    of my hollow.

May the pit be filled
by the sound of lips.

FOR MOHMOH

When I remember you, I remember us—
      two boys running around the front
yard, our mothers' voices like arrows that
      do not wound but halt. And soon we'd
stop chasing, the dust falling on our little feet.
      I fear this is all I have left of you—
memory so frail, it cannot weave you back.
      On the day of your death, I wept but
barely enough. Perhaps I was too young for
      grief, my sorrow too fleeting to be named
sorrow. I think of you now and I can hear a
      pattering, like a quick pelt on the roof of
my heart. I imagine those are your feet still
      running, so I drum my fingers against my
chest, pretending to follow you again.

THE CLOCKS
for Jude

They buried my friend, my
lovely friend, and the clocks

did not mourn him. Time
did not kneel. August

wilted without cease.
It did not even rain the day

he died, all heat and blinding
shine. You, dumb weather.

I did not need your light.
Nothing better than

monsoons and melancholy.
Of what use is light

if it fails to brighten
a grave? There are some

glooms that refuse to be
pierced—the rays touch

the darkness and become it.
Stupid sun, you multiply

my sorrow. See, my heart,
impermeable. On its surface,

layers of black stack.
It is September, dear friend,

and nothing has changed.
The winds still blow as if

you, too, weren't made
of wind. I refuse to agree

the world does not owe us
sympathy. I want to walk

in the fields and see your
face all over the greens.

I want your soft voice
to dwell inside the rain.

APPLYING PSALMS 121 TO AN UNBELIEVER

Some years ago, I began shredding
my tongue, crumbling the chapel

once built in my mouth.   I retired
my eyes watching the hills—they sang,

*help will somebody water down, but daily
I died of thirst.*   Once, I tried to fetch God

with language; my voice—white ink
stitching white paper.   There were no

angels to color my ache.   Perhaps
I'm oblivious to the dialect of heaven,

I gave God a wound to heal and he placed
a ribbon around the bleed.   As if to say,

*look at your blood, pray and it will blue into
a stream.*   But I do not know what to

weave from faith.   Prayer reminds me
what absence tethers me from.

When I fold myself to kneel as a saint,
a lily wilts before my teeth.   As if to say,

*crawl to your mother's feet and confess your
unbelief.*   How do I say I am a church bell

swaying without its tongue?   Her heart—
a holy book my chaos must not set on fire.

HOMECOMING

Sorry I killed the flowers, Ma. They were
so pretty. But we were not going to eat them.
Forgive me. I sound so cavalier. I promise I am
softer than my horns. It's just difficult to imagine
any kind of beauty, with such hunger quaking
my bones. After seven months, I returned home.
My family had turned the house into a terrible
garden—green and pink chaos sprawled all over
the front yard. I asked Ma why this happened.
She smiled with her eyes, then said something
about money and growing our own food. I could
reason with that. We had so little. But the ground
was so much. So fertile, our pockets could afford
not to starve. So, when I took the hoe, startling
the amber frog hiding in the bushes, I spared
the other plants: the vegetables, the beans, the
red peppers, the corns—oh, especially the corns.
We would boil or roast them during those cold
evenings. I spared them, but no, not the flowers.
Will you ever forgive me, Ma? The weeds were
choking them anyway.

WHITE NOISE APARTMENT

What doesn't irritate
me these days? Even

my shadow, the body's
evidence, is disturbance.

But we can tolerate light
since we cannot hear it.

Graceful thing. Bless
your silence. The way

you move through a body,
needless of orchestra.

With sound, I cannot find
a compromise. Not in this

apartment. No thrush can
live here. It will leap

to nest somewhere gentle,
free from sharp chatter,

where the loudest voice
in the room is its own chirp.

Like any lost child,
I want to go home. I miss

the peace of familiar blood,
the smell of my solitude

circling around. But I do
not have these anymore.

Here, white noise prevails.
Everyone's always screaming

something at something,
screaming at something

delicate. The bird in me
cannot survive this. I am

too velvety for collision,
physical or sonic.

Bring me a room

that doesn't threaten
with tongues—voices

void of swords. A church
without the violence

of vespers. Let every noise
strike my bone, then

waft through it without
percussion. I desire pure

calm. The aura of
nothing. The sound of

diamonds crackling at the
ocean floor. The boatman

cannot hear it. The wood,
gliding across the water's

quiet skin. Give me stillness
like that. Soft ripple of blue.

FEAR IS THE BOY'S SAVIOR

Heck, it is never
the flesh that seeks death. The body loves itself

too much. Even when a knife
presses into a wrist, the veins rebel against

the metal, hold it, first, before they allow.
It is anatomy saying, *we were not built for hurt*,

proof the body is its own shield.

Often, I have wondered
how to flee and flee softly. To do it and do it quiet.

To leave the instrument clean, the exit bloodless
as a fossil. Really, there should be a simpler

way to it: without nuance, unceremonious, like
a pull that releases a lace. Doesn't all that color

terrify? I am afraid of leaving behind
blood. No, I will not disturb the vein.

Inside my trembling, a whisper:
Sheathe the knife, it says. And the coward will live

because he is obedient to his fright.
I will live because I am obedient to my fright.

HYPOTHESIS

How stupid, dependent, is ache that it needs
the body to exist. Weak thing without form.
Reveal yourself.

Hypothesis: agony is so frail,
we cannot touch it.

When Mother sought after wellness in a
chapel, she carried me and my brothers along.
I remember, once, the prophet asked me,

Are you a Christian?

And I wondered if my faux faith was the
hindrance to her miracle. When I arrived
home, I sainted myself clean as a dove.

Hypothesis: love will make a man
trade unbelief for healing.

Each morning, we sang *glory*. And nothing
changed. We sang *glory*. And the wound spread
further. *Glory*. And the wound glorified itself.

Hypothesis: faith is suffering, mistranslated.

During a sermon, the prophet's wife says
tribulation is the heirloom of the earth;
only in heaven shall we find eternal peace.

Invention: heaven is wherever I say it is.
I point at my mother's illness and it whitens.

TONGUES

> *Ọlọrun, fun iya mi ni ilera to dara.*

Not even the language of the prophets can rain down a miracle from the sky. I have watched, years upon years, litanies ricocheting off her skin. Do you not wonder how the pious can be filled with so much plague? The irony laughs, as if mocking us. The clergy, the greatest lie.

> *Why have you forsaken us?*

She is bedridden again, and I am here, helpless in my hope. O cursed be the predictability of compassion. That words are incapable of healing means language forsakes.

> *Lord, keep her alive. Bless her bones with the rhapsody of light.*

"For she said within herself, if I may but touch his garment, I shall be whole." —Matthew 9:21

Not once, not twice, her hands have held onto the fabric, clenched, seeking to squeeze grace out of the threads. Yet not even a drop blessed her palms. But what faith was absent in the fingers that touched? What sin keeps shielding the body from its rapture? Comforter, will you not teach us the physics of healing? How to tongue a prayer that will not lead us to confusion.

SURRENDERING TO LOVE

I used to hide the things that
caused me wreck. If I adored you,

    I would bury my dirges, and instead,
    offer you a song made of honey.

Liken me to a lantern that limns a room,
while all of its insides slowly burn.

    Is it not magnificent how one
    can give light, yet hold a furnace

trapped inside the chest? At times
the trick is difficult to pull off.

    Once, I was speaking with a friend.
    I tried so much to mask my worry;

    She looked at me and asked,
    why did you salten your face?

I could feel all around my throat,
orchids stitching, my mouth

    a field of vines wrestling my
    tongue. When I finally spoke,

I said, *last night, a fountain broke
out of me.* She kissed my cheeks—

       blessed rapture of skin—
    and for those seconds, I could

not name my sadness, could
not even remember its genesis.

    Perhaps all I always needed
    was an arm to unspool into,

not the pity of the eye,
but the love of the lip.

    I am learning that the only
       way to healing is to lay bare,

that the fire, like the wound,
should be tended to.

    I swear by the cobalt blue,
I will surrender to love.

ACKNOWLEDGMENTS

Much gratitude to the editors of the following publications where these poems first appeared:

Afapinen: "Flight"
Frontier Poetry: "For Mohmoh"
Leavings Lit Mag: "Applying Psalms 121 to an Unbeliever"
The poems "Tongues" and "Hypothesis" first appeared in the chapbook *Heaven Is a Metaphor.*